2/15

D1524716

Yorkipoos

by Ruth Owen

PowerKiDS press™

New York

Published in 2015 by The Rosen Publishing Group, Inc.
29 East 21st Street, New York, NY 10010

Copyright © 2015 by The Rosen Publishing Group, Inc.

First Edition

Produced for Rosen by Ruby Tuesday Books Ltd
Editor for Ruby Tuesday Books Ltd: Mark J. Sachner
US Editor: Joshua Shadowens
Designer: Emma Randall

Photo Credits:
Cover, 3, 4 (left), 4 (center), 5, 6–7, 8–9, 10–11, 12–13, 14–15, 16, 19 (top), 20–21, 26, 28–29, 30 © Shutterstock; 1, 17, 19 (bottom) © Istockphoto; 4 (right), 22–23, 24–25, 27 © Warren Photographic.

Library of Congress Cataloging-in-Publication Data

Owen, Ruth, 1967– author.
 Yorkipoos / by Ruth Owen. — 1st ed.
    pages cm. — (Designer dogs)
 Includes index.
 ISBN 978-1-4777-7035-1 (library binding) — ISBN 978-1-4777-7036-8 (pbk.) — ISBN 978-1-4777-7037-5 (6-pack)
 1. Yorkie poo—Juvenile literature. 2. Toy dogs—Juvenile literature. 3. Dogs—Juvenile literature. I. Title.
 SF429.Y57O94 2015
 636.76—dc23

2014004538

Manufactured in the United States of America

CPSIA Compliance Information: Batch #WS14PK8: For Further Information contact Rosen Publishing, New York, New York at 1-800-237-9932

Contents

Meet a Yorkipoo

What is teeny tiny, super smart, has bundles of energy, and a gorgeous silky coat? The answer is a yorkipoo.

A yorkipoo is a cross, or mixture, of two different dog **breeds**. This type of dog is known as a **crossbreed** dog. When a Yorkshire terrier and a poodle have puppies together, they make yorkipoos.

Yorkipoos belong to a dog group called toy dogs. Toy dogs are small dogs whose main job is to be **companions** to people.

Adult Yorkshire terrier

Adult poodle

Yorkipoo puppy

An adult yorkipoo

The name "yorkipoo" is made up from the names "Yorkshire terrier" and "poodle."

5

What Is a Designer Dog?

People have been **breeding** different types of dogs for thousands of years.

Some dog breeds were created to be working dogs. These dogs were bred to herd sheep or cattle. Some breeds helped hunters track and catch rabbits. Many small dog breeds were created to be pet dogs.

In the past 20 to 30 years, dog **breeders** have created some new dog breeds that are nicknamed "designer dogs." These breeds, such as yorkipoos, are called designer dogs because breeders designed them from two existing breeds.

A yorkipoo puppy might have a poodle mom and a Yorkshire terrier dad, or a terrier mom and poodle dad.

A black and tan-colored yorkipoo puppy

A black adult yorkipoo

Meet the Parents: Yorkshire Terriers

Yorkshire terriers, or Yorkies as they are often called, are a toy dog breed. These little dogs are brave, have lots of energy, and love to investigate new things. Yorkies have a huge doggie personality squeezed into a tiny body that weighs less than 7 pounds (3 kg).

Many Yorkie owners have their dogs' coats clipped, or trimmed short. If the hair is left to get long, it will be straight, shiny, and very silky. A Yorkie's coat is golden brown and a dark gray color, called steel blue.

Adult Yorkshire terrier size

Height to shoulder: 8 to 9 inches (20–23 cm)

8

A Yorkie with a long coat

The American Kennel Club is a club for dog breeders. Each year, the club makes a list of how many dogs are owned in each breed. In 2013, Yorkies were the sixth most popular breed on the list, out of 177 different breeds.

Meet the Parents: Yorkie Rat Catchers

Terriers are usually small breeds of dogs that were bred for catching animals such as rats, rabbits, and foxes. Today's Yorkshire terriers are mostly **pampered** pups that live as companion dogs. Their **ancestors**, however, were working dogs.

Yorkshire terriers get their name because they were first bred in the county of Yorkshire in England. In the 1800s, these dogs were used to catch rats in mills that made clothing and other products from cotton and wool.

A Yorkie is always on the lookout to have fun with its terrier hunting skills.

Yorkies have never forgotten that they were once rat-catching dogs. Today's pet Yorkshire terriers love to hunt for toys, or even chase small animals in their yards!

A ball isn't a rat, but it's a close second!

Meet the Parents: Poodles

Poodles are smart companion dogs that love to learn new things and show off their tricks!

Poodles are just one breed of dog, but they come in three different sizes. A large poodle that measures over 15 inches (38 cm) to the shoulder is called a standard poodle. The smaller miniature poodle measures between 10 and 15 inches (25–38 cm) to the shoulder. The tiny toy poodle measures less than 10 inches (25 cm). Yorkipoos usually have a miniature or a toy poodle as their mom or dad.

A black poodle

A white poodle

A poodle's curly hair feels a little like wool. Its coat can be black, gray, silver, white, red, or apricot.

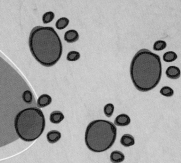

A gray poodle

An apricot poodle

A silver poodle

A red poodle

Meet the Parents: Water Poodles

Poodles were first bred in Germany. These working dogs helped their owners hunt ducks and other water birds. Once a bird was shot, the poodle dove into the pond or lake, retrieved the dead bird, and carried it back to its owner.

Working poodles spent lots of time in water, so a special poodle hairstyle was invented. In this style, the poodle's body was mostly hair free. Some puffy sections of hair were left, however, to keep the dog's joints and important **organs** warm. Some owners still clip their poodles in this style today.

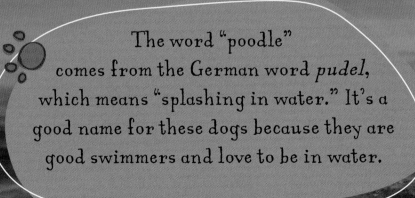

The word "poodle" comes from the German word *pudel*, which means "splashing in water." It's a good name for these dogs because they are good swimmers and love to be in water.

A standard poodle with its coat clipped into puffy shapes

15

Sneeze-Free Pooches

Unfortunately, many people have trouble being around dogs because they are **allergic** to the animals. Most dogs shed, or drop, their hair. The hair carries tiny bits of dead skin called dander. Dog dander can make an allergic person sneeze, have trouble breathing, or get sore, itchy skin.

Poodles do not shed their hair, however, so many allergic people do not get ill when they are with a poodle. Dog breeders created many designer dog breeds using poodles. These "poo" or "doodle" breeds, such as yorkipoos, can be a safe pet choice for people with allergies.

A labradoodle

One of the first sneeze-free designer dog breeds to be created was the labradoodle. Breeders mixed a Labrador retriever with a poodle.

A yorkipoo

Yorkipoo Looks

Some adult yorkipoos weigh only 3 pounds (1.4 kg) and measure just 7 inches (18 cm) to their shoulders. Others are bigger, weighing up to 14 pounds (6.4 kg) and measuring just over 1 foot (30 cm).

Just like its Yorkie parent, a yorkipoo has super soft, silky hair. The hair can be straight, wavy, or curly.

Yorkipoos may be black, chocolate-brown, tan, cream, gray, silver, white, red, apricot, or mixed colors. They often get their colors from their colorful poodle parents!

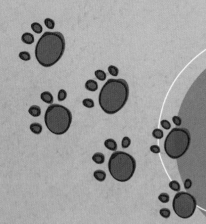

A yorkipoo usually gets its size from its poodle parent. If the poodle was a toy, the yorkipoo will be tiny. If the poodle parent was a miniature, the yorkipoo will be larger.

A poodle

A Yorkshire terrier

This yorkipoo looks like a mixture of its parents' breeds.

Yorkipoo Personalities

A yorkipoo has two loves in its life—its owners and having fun!

These little pups live to give love and want to spend lots of time cuddled up on their owners' laps. When it comes to playtime, however, they are bundles of energy that can run fast and jump high.

Poodles and Yorkshire terriers are both smart dog breeds. So when you put them together, you get super smart yorkipoos that are quick to learn and easy to train.

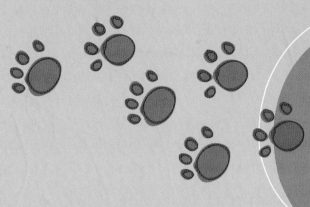

Yorkipoos love to learn and perform tricks in return for treats. These dogs never get tired of having fun. Even senior yorkipoos still like to show off all the tricks they know.

There's just so much fun to be had!

Yorkipoo Puppies

Yorkipoos are usually born in a **litter** of four to six puppies.

The newborn puppies cannot walk, and their eyes are tightly shut. The little brothers and sisters spend their days snuggled together asleep. When they wake up, they drink milk from their poodle or Yorkshire terrier mom.

Just four weeks later, however, the pups are very active. Their eyes have opened and they can run, play, wag their tails, and bark.

At about four to five weeks old, yorkipoo puppies begin to eat solid food. They try special canned puppy food and bowls of cereal with milk. Mom's milk is still their favorite food, though.

A six-week-old yorkipoo puppy

Dad poodle

Mom Yorkshire terrier

Lots to Learn

Yorkipoo pups must stay with their mom and brothers and sisters until they are at least eight weeks old. Spending these first weeks of their lives with their doggie family is very important because the puppies learn a lot for the future.

The puppies chase and play fight. This helps the pups learn how to use their bodies—just like a child playing a sport. If a puppy bites its mom, the mom dog will tell her naughty baby off. Then the puppy learns that biting is not OK.

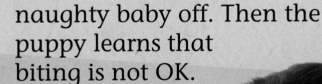

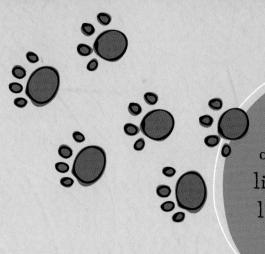

A yorkipoo's personality begins to show at about six weeks old. One pup in a litter might be a rough-and-tough little bruiser. Another pup might be very gentle and shy.

The yorkipoo pups in a litter can all look very different.

Caring for a Yorkipoo

The tiny yorkipoo puppy that you buy from a dog breeder, may live for up to 15 years. That's lots of years of love and care that you must give your dog.

A yorkipoo has lots of energy, so it needs a walk every day. Playing an energetic game of fetch in your backyard, or even a hallway in your home, works, too.

A yorkipoo's silky coat gets easily tangled. So the dog's hair must be brushed every day to keep it in top condition.

A yorkipoo will grow to his or her adult size in about a year. The young dog will still act and think like a puppy until it is about two years old, though.

This six-week-old yorkipoo pup is not much bigger than a guinea pig!

Little Dog, Big Dog?

A yorkipoo's terrier history can make it act like one **feisty** little dog.

Yorkipoos don't seem to realize how tiny they are. Sometimes, they pick fights with much bigger dogs! They can also accidentally get hurt during rough games with bigger playmates. Therefore, a yorkipoo's owner should carefully introduce the little dog to any new doggie friends, and always stay nearby.

Yorkipoos just love to bark, and bark, and bark. When someone knocks on the door, a yorkipoo will bravely bark to guard its home.

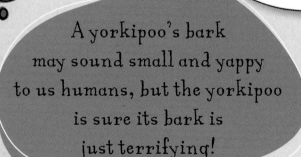

WOOF! GRRR!

A yorkipoo's bark may sound small and yappy to us humans, but the yorkipoo is sure its bark is just terrifying!

Glossary

allergic (A-lur-jik)
Reacting badly to something, such as an animal or type of food. A person who is allergic to something may sneeze, get sore skin, vomit, or become seriously ill.

ancestors
(AN-ses-terz) Relatives who lived long ago.

breeders
(BREE-derz)
People who breed animals, such as dogs, and sell them.

breeding
(BREED-ing)
Putting a male and a female animal together so they mate and have young.

breeds (BREEDZ)
Different types of dogs or other animals.

crossbreed (KROS-breed) A type of dog created from two different breeds.

litter (LIH-ter) A group of baby animals all born to the same mother at the same time.

companions (kum-PAN-yunz) People or animals with whom one spends a lot of time.

organs (OR-genz) Body parts, such as the heart and lungs, that have particular jobs to do.

feisty (FY-stee) Lively, brave, and willing to take care of oneself.

pampered (PAM-purd) Treated with much care and attention.

Websites
Due to the changing nature of Internet links, PowerKids Press has developed an online list of websites related to the subject of this book. This site is updated regularly. Please use this link to access the list:

www.powerkidslinks.com/ddog/york/

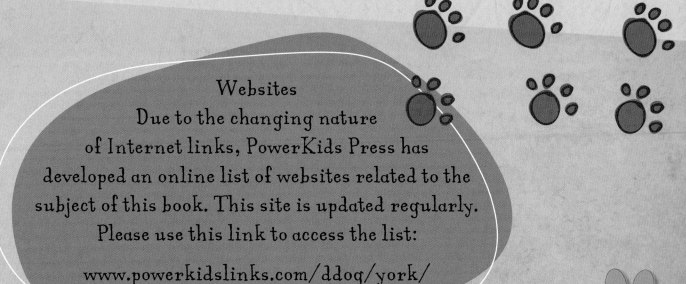

Read More

Beal, Abigail. *I Love My Yorkshire Terrier.* Top Dogs. New York: PowerKids Press, 2011.

Mathea, Heidi. *Poodles.* Dogs. Minneapolis, MN: Checkerboard Books, 2011.

Wilsdon, Christina. *Dogs.* Amazing Animals. New York: Gareth Stevens, 2009.

Index